The Darndest Dictionary

By Mark Namsick

It's not a reference book,
but you can refer to it if you want.

Published in Comic Sans to be more readable if
dyslexic.   Everyone else is on their own.

ISBN: 978-0-692-88516-1
© 2017 Mark Namsick   All Rights Reserved.
Cover Photo by Alice Achterhof

Preface

"The beginning of wisdom is
the definition of terms."
- Socrates

According to Socrates, saying a word without understanding its meaning succeeds only in making meaningless noise. This idea had a strong impact on my early years. To see that some concepts like love or beauty could take a lifetime to partially define was humbling.

I soon realized that looking up "meaning" in the dictionary was not the shortcut to living a meaningful life, and looking up "morality" was not useful for being moral. This made me wonder often about the meaning of words, all the while adding to my own list of definitions. A love of music provided a sense of rhyme, interplay, poetic qualities and connotation.

Eventually I realized there was much more to words than could ever be put together in a "real" dictionary, and that writing one would be futile to attempt.

This is that attempt.

And it rhymes.

Accident

Happenstance of quantum things
or pluck of luck to puppet strings.

Accompaniment

A you to be beside a me
to be a we in harmony.

Advertisement

An overpass of comprehension
built to span a short attention.

Anger

The trying sound of pain
as it tries to leave the brain.
What's expelled must then be felt,
so often we retain.

Ambition

A commodity kept in stock in every store:
more and more, and more and more.

Apathy

Were I to wear a warning
the sign would simply say:
I had three fucks this morning
but I gave them all away.

Appear

To vanish in reverse;
a line of sight traverse.

Aspire

To throw a grapple of the mind
to where you want to start to climb.

Archaeologist

He who pines to smell a fine perfume
once upon a time he might exhume.

Autodidact

A self-made man who taught himself -
no help but those who loaded screen and shelf.

Animals

All of us a cousin of em'.

Autopsy

To peel and part my parts in part to see
if perhaps a person murdered me.

Average Joe

The median man, often not
a go-getter that ever greatly got.

Battlefield

What politicians put upon
a soldier left to soldier on.

Beauty

The whole surpassing sum of parts,
as separate strokes mingle
to a single
piece
of
art.

Bias

Wind which blows your mind ashore.
Every ship resigned to drift
finds itself a derelict, no more.

Bicycle

A pulley made to push.
A brake that's meant to rush.
Oh to go for half an hour
by pedal, gear and flour power.

Birth

Mature or pre evacuation,
post mature or pre ejaculation.

Blanket

A curtain of cotton
blown by winds
of worlds forgotten.

Blasphemy

To go against the holy bible
in spirit, for in print it's libel.

Blouse

A top to stop the light revealing
what we're taught demands concealing.
Covers not the face but shames the breast;
the accepted burka of the west.

Border

The boundary those within
are all-in and bout about.

Book Bag

A bag of nooks to bag your books today
which Kindle wants to whisk away.

Break Up

Pry apart the part attained
to start a broken heart again.

Bridge

Stepping stone beyond compare:
a short-cut cut through open air.

Bull

A beast which feasts as we await
the shit that's his to delegate.

Bus

Fraternity which daily changes,
membership and destinations.

Caffeine

More imbibed when less alert
so think not hurt.

Caller I.D.

Unwanted callers christened;
a catalyst for cell division.

Calorie

A bit of your mizzle, before it's the shizzle.

Cannibals

Contrarians elite
that eat the meat
of vegetarians.

Cannonball

As the earth, a metal ball.
Once spring has sprung then all is fall.

Car

Creationists insist
it's a contrivance that drives us.

Carbon

Weightless while exhausting and it seems
to warm the world to smithereens.

Catholics

Beatles fans who coo and fawn
under Paul, and over John.

Ceiling

A blockade made for warming,
or glass barrier alarming
when used for keeping people down,
not miniature farming.

Cemetery

Fickle fates our futures jot,
putting pits in lots of plots.

Censors

Men of class few words get past
who'd never mention gas
except in passing.

Chain

A bit of clink to link a given length of links to things.

Chair

This stand can stand to bear your end
'til you can bear to stand again.

Charity

What some got,
and won't, but ought.

Chicken

A bitty bird we've often bit to bones;
purposeful when crossing roads.

Choice

To publicly contrive who lives and dies
or hang the hidden hangers up to dry.

Church

Where many people share one heart,
hand in hand, and set apart.

Circle

Any path which deviates a little
finds beginning after middle.

Clairvoyant

One who sees enough to meddle
only once the dust is settled.

Clock

An eye to watch the sun go by
despite a door or darkened sky.

Concrete

Fact of which there is no contestation,
set in stone by mixture with precipitation.

Conjugal

The modern con has visitation
to beat the rap and grant probation.

Constantine

Bestowed upon a billion people
a wild throne and broken steeple.

Consummation

Well-earned success is better than sex,
though non-validation beats masturbation.

Comedy

A beautiful fool stumbles into
happiness and fortune glue.

Computer

A billion bits of somethings
switching microscopic lights which brighten
screens, show what more ones and zeroes than
we've ever seen, are supposed to really mean.

Constellation

Distant dots which push and pull,
empty out, and swallow whole.

Corporation

A little cell holding little people's lives,
endlessly metastasized.

Cow

A beast of burden brown of eyes,
atop a plate, aside of fries.

Crime

Sin apparent to a vast majority
or good fun spoiled by someone in authority.
That which you may not,
but some do and get caught,
though often a minority.

Cruelty

Suffering contagious
to turn inside outrageous.

Crumb

As ice is to berg so crumb is to bread;
a burgerberg ahoy ahead.

Cry

To look inside for all to see,
and brave the private publicly.

Cunnilingus

Lend your man a hand and do not frown,
for who comes up must then go down.

Cunning

Undertaking aftermath
and cognizant of consequence.

Cup

A lip to keep a dozen sips of stuff
from dripping down and messing up.

Cupid

Pierces hearty arteries,
hardened as Achilles was to archery.

Current

Magnets spun can make electrons be
powerfully slippery.

Dagger

A long-abused and short antique
once sprung a trap to spring a leak.

Dancing

Merely granting one or more
a more than ordinary measure
of your full attention.

Darkness

A Luddite putting up a fight,
'gainst the yawning of the night.

Death

Your father's father is father fodder,
the stuff of stuff we self-explore;
the you that was before you were
forever is, and are no more.

Democracy

A brain contains a kingdom,
and every king decrees
sentiment or logic
and little in-between.
I bid you bid that despot part
with power over mind or heart
so great debates and passions sway
to bring tomorrow to today.

Diamond

Soot that wasn't satisfied
'til time and tension rarefied.

Disagreement

Won by point of fact or tip of sword;
censorship, or better written word.

Discretion

To hush and shush and trip a trap
which desperately wants to yap.

Download

Duplicate a little bit;
a copy of a counterfeit.

Drama

Stress and mess to clean and dress
each cut and scrape this life begets.

Drug

A lever sending pain and pleasure
out of order just in order to
be short reformer of the former;
underground if overdo.

Dualism

A major meme that always seems
to mean a couple different things.

Dust

Just a crust, but one we cling to oft,
as rust we must be once we shuffle off.

Ear

A keyhole through which things are rampant,
which to eyes are not apparent,
making sense of those events which hid
from groping hand and gaping lid.

Edit

Take a bit of wood and nail,
add a rudder, mast and sail.

Ejaculate

To vent frustrations;
the ramifications
of tense relations.

Ellipse

Three periods to start a pause,
grammatical menarche à trios.

Emotion

Big pictures of quantum chances;
quarks react, and fire dances.

Entendre

Intoxicants to blur your view,
dividing vision or cognition into two,
whether extra wine imbibed or thought imbued.

Enterprise

A project propelled by people who surround it,
though actually it's space that warps around it.

Epitaph

A private era none but you has known,
briefly put, and set in stone.

Epitome

An epiphany to see
I'm the epitome of me.
All that else can ever be
is just a it of you and we.

Equation

An abstract construction
with numbers for lumber.

Esophagus

A soup of sort-of former food
squeezes down this tooth-paste tube.

Euphemism

Superfluous syllables spoke to misdirect
from that which might yourself reflect.

Evangelist

A viral file thought it might
folder label over-write.

Explosion

Phenomenon emergent,
both uniform and urgent.

Fart

When three are in an elevator
the source of their displeasure
as any carpenter knows well,
but once you cut
and twice you measure.

Father

A parent apparently,
maybe inherently.

Father Time

Slow and steady moves the glacier
makin' time with mother nature.

Fear

Small cudgel that bludgeons
all noggins it nudges.

Fellatio

As any penis punished will assert
comeuppance can be just dessert.

Fertile

Fit to plant a plant to
make another plant to
till and till
until you will
a blue pill need to plan to.

Fiction

Right to write
what's not but might,
or won't but still
your heart excites.

Fire

Breaking chains which never brake until
every bond has broken, or every link is still.

Fission

The saddest of all matters is
the loneliness of matter, 'tis
a fact when atoms come together,
hearts are one, then bonds are severed.

Flash

A sudden blinding sense of whiteness
as if by something nude and Irish.

Flood

What God did self-prohibit
lest he loose the holy spigot.

Foam

An atom's view far from home,
of its and many other domes.

Food

Fuel for thought without which we halt,
best ingested with a grain or two of salt.

Fog

Sometimes the sea grows stormy,
and makes the seaways horny.

Forgive

To love in light of
and in spite of.

Fortune

After all he oughtn't mind
the won and lost, the more aware
that every step which fate assigned
led him to him, and brought you there.

Frankenstein

Maker of a monstrous dummy.
Feared by all, except his mummy.

Friend

One whose where's the same as you
just so there's the two of you.

Fundamentalist

On the path of parables he sees
not the moral of the forest,
but the fiction in the trees.

Gas Chamber

Where one may find the guilt of crime
in of door, and out of time.

Gerrymandering

Why half the leaders you abhor
are not the droids you voted for.

Ginger

Red head or brown bread;
each speck a freckle, or raisin fed.

Glass

A magic crystal which may without conception,
reflect on your and pass on my perception.

God

Proof of which is hard to show.
He must exist; we cannot know.

Government

A force for solving all our problems
assuming that it did not cause them.

Granted

Given, but worth so much more
than we receive when taken for.

Graze

When fauna feed upon on a floor of flora.

Gunshot

Small tears in sound barriers
to tear a mother's little ones away from her.

Hair

A euphemism for the fur adorning
apes who mourn and scorn their origins.
A rose by any name would smell as sweet,
even springing from the mud beneath your feet.

Halloween

Two tons of sweets to feed me
to two types of diabetes.

Hate

The moment pain or alarm
push to wish or act of harm.

Heartbreak

Humpty Dumpty waits beyond
a wall called love he'd set upon;
'til a passerby impart
pieces from an eggshell heart.

Home

Any other people who
ever feel at home with you.

Hospital

The only church which once admits,
binds the wound, and then remits.

House

A giant splinter that remains
until the loan has been regained.

Hurricane

Wind and hail that hails from far away;
circling the halo of a vast tornado.

Hypocrisy

A second splinter we acquire
eye to eye, discerning neither.

Idealism

An isle of hell that lies between
All Is Well, and All We've Seen.
Those who'll only see one shore
condemn us thus forevermore.

Idolatry

A finger pointed to the sky
at burning sun or cooling rain,
deciding which to petrify,
'til life is gone and stone remains.

Ignorance

Not to know is not a sin;
a circle all are born within.
But to believe you are without,
is to pretend without a doubt.

Indoctrinate

Encourage and anoint
a child to play for points,
perhaps one day to play no more
and find no one was keeping score.

Inessential

Needlessly abundant,
superfluous, and redundant.

Infidel

An adulteress arrested
for that which has offended
a patriarch to whom her heart
had never been intended.

Inflation

Bankers make and break a mint
when gold is green and fit to print.

Immortality

A gift denied to man and Adam,
while granted to his every atom.

Jacket

A coat to coat, quote-unquote.

Jesus

Concurrently enforced and banned;
the most noted and mis-quoted man.

Jettison

Discard that which you've collected,
but no longer want, or have digested.

Joseph

A foretold cuckold.

Jury Duty

Waive the right to represent
and give consent to circumvent.

Justice

Truth will out to those within
ear and shout of reasonable doubt.

Kill

Take a beautiful machine
and introduce a wrench
to break all it has ever been,
save a motive for revenge.

Law

Three way split 'tween he who is I am,
mother earth, and uncle sam.

Lefty

The sort of sort to turn to port.

Lesbian

She who knows just where it's at,
bit for bit, 'n' tit for tat.

Lexicographer

One who until now defined
words in ways which didn't rhyme.

Life

A puzzle that muddles heart and eye;
solutions found by all
but those who never try.

Light

The filmy residue that's left upon your sight,
after scouring the night.

Living

A most persistent thorny weed -
clutch it tight and fingers bleed.
Let it go to drop the pain,
and pick up naught but ought again.

LOL

Reaction when a leg somebody pulls,
though often compensating for the lulls.

Love

Pain and pleasure I could not define
by the hundredth page of word and rhyme.

Lose

Back to square one or two
where everything's the same - but you.

Marketing

Smiling widely calm and coldly,
right hand reaching in a hat
retrieves a rabbit, now watch closely;
you had this, and I have that.

Marriage

To pray away the gaiety
and make two people whole
to friend and foe and family
in every blended role.

Martyr

Hoped and loved and set upon,
dream dispelled and love withdrawn,
slipped the grip of guardian hand,
and left behind to carry on.

Mary

Live a life of love inerrant,
still end up a teenage parent.

Mine

Owned, but only rented
once the patent's pended.

Miss

Move beyond, continue forward
intending to have traveled toward.

Morality

Values which objectively
coincide subjectively.

Mortal

Once upon a didn't happen
a salesman tempted Eve and Adam;
with serpent's oil said to cure
the very thing they always were.

Motorcycle

The seed who speeds and hurries hardest
halves the time to fall and harvest.

Movie

A thousand million pictures still,
fired rapid fire 'til
they overtake our real world perception.
Reality and fiction blur
as we prefer
whichever has the best direction.

Multiverse

Our existence would be lonely
if it was the one and only.

Mystery

Nature gave us eyes to tease us
just to tempt to search and please us.

Narcissism

Stretching mirrors;
shards and slivers.

Necrophilia

A pervert's private parts interred
in one who was not twice disturbed.

Neighborhood

Lots of lots of little things
of broken homes and makeshift dreams;
a kingdom where a child king begins
to conquer hope and fear and then
leaves to face the world unknown,
and doesn't quite return again.

News

Focus the people's collective attention
on what few tycoons selectively mention.

No

Sometimes a Yes whose shrewd disguise
is infiltrated through the eyes.

Not

Love this life of lovely-nots,
woo the world of never-be,
because for all her many faults
she found a place for you and me.

Number

A symbol defining a unit,
a quantity, weight or a cubit,
extent or degree,
or the latest draftee
the Yankees had thought would be prudent.

Oblivious

Cut the lawn and cook the food
for decades, but inquire
not to how the grass renewed,
or what in hell was fire.

Omega

In ancient Greece, a modern zed
which means a Z to me instead.

OMG

Rarely spoke in open air.
Like totally the shortest prayer.

Open

Pried wide, as eye or mind.
I do adore a door to more
than we have time to find.

Order

The sequence of events you're told
you must commence lest someone scold.

Ours

Held as hands, or take in turn;
investment of the best return.

Oxygen

Fuel which if not constantly consumed,
a candle flickers, and darkness looms.

Paint

A theory of conspiracy does bid
a whistle to blow open wide the lid,
of a cover up that covers,
something hidden from us, nebulous -
but spruced up something's prob'ly all it did.

Particle

The stuff the stuff is made up of.

Passion

Thoughts are for carefully collecting
while feelings are peeling off the ceiling.

Patronize

Become accustomed to bestow
custom unto one below.

Peace

If un-swung one oughtn't swing
the business end of anything.

Pen

A squid obscures the foes which it engages,
be they fish, or empty pages.

Penny

A bit of shiny copper worth a tiny nearly naught;
lucky plucked when lost, and sold for thoughts.

Perfect

Just so; even though
your ideal's my so-so.

Person

Blood and gut and feeling,
heart and head concealing,
'til mouth or cheek
spring a leak,
a universe revealing.

Philosopher

An ancient word for nerd.
Brings to mind a time when few were found
who thought and taught and gathered 'round.

Phone

A camera which connects the masses,
finds your way, and does your taxes.

Planet

Solar puppets dance about their strings
casting shadows out which go unseen.

Plastique

An adjustable combustible.

Poetry

A trail of crumb to tempt a mind
to look and seek, explore and find
what before your eye had been expressed,
and what behind is now confessed.

Pope

Father to the children of creation;
or a political administration.

Pornographer

Purveyor of performance arts
with casting calls for private parts.

Prejudice

A vantage from me to you.
The point where I was born
and all my eyes could view.

Problem

Were solutions as we wish them be,
simple and magical, never would we
lesson learn, or student be.

Progress

Greener grass he's going toward,
apple fall, and tumble forward.

Prophet

Submitted patents pending
rubber-stamping reinventing.

Punctuated Equilibrium

Hopeful monsters on the hill
climbed to find themselves until
one day one fell, and carried hope away
with wings it took a spill to splay.

Quarter

A half a half is half and not;
25 in coin, and half in thought.

Quest

A noble search to distant plains;
pajamas rich with Cheeto stains.

Quilt

Took the time to bind with string
effort went and comfort bring.

Quit

To choose to lose, or end an overuse
of that which now does not amuse.

Radio

A universe of beauty we can't see,
until attuned by love and wound
unto the proper frequency.

Rain

When a pregnant water body drains,
the sky comes down with sympathy pains.

Rainbow

The spectrum seen as all inclusive,
though black and white do seem elusive.

Randy

A name bestowed by those who named,
nine months past they were the same.

React

To be equal in opposition,
absent of your own volition.

Reassure

To show a heart that knows again
that in its ears were only fears;
whisperings of malcontent
felt as meant, for many years.

Recommit

To adore some more may mend amore.

Reform

Adjust a jot or tittle to
improve a lot, or little do.

Reincarnate

Sacred cow does see a light,
opening of tunnel bright.
Re-cast to play a pungent role
beyond this bowl for passing souls.

Reptile

Hatched from whom it had no say;
over with, and underway.

Résumé

The raised skirt and roadside naked knee
of a working class economy.

Right

On the one hand the opposite of left,
and on the other one the only choice that's left
if all the others are perverse.
Which leaves the third:
a forgotten soldier's end
and remembered debt incurred.

Rimming

To sanctify a holy thing
which hopefully is sparkling.

Ritual

Willful effort will assign
worth in one's unconscious mind.

Road

We whine away the time in DMV,
in which we wait, to wait in line in SUV.

Romantic

That which makes a heart beat fast,
body still, and question asked.

Sacred

An enemy in the making when
one cannot hope to make amends,
once against it he offends.

Salmon

A fin to go, a fin to stay,
an effin' waterfall to lay.

Sand

Grit to mark each eon as it passes;
granules in grand canyon hourglasses.

Science

Set a spell upon a tree
of knowledge ever after,
thereupon did Isaac see
an apple fall, and gathered.

Scripture

A man of mystery, worlds apart
every moral did impart,
ghost-written in assistant's hand;
vicarious divine commands.

Seat Belt

Strips of straps to bar your bones
from being thrown by known unknowns.

Second

A paradox I reckoned,
as the first was also second.

Sensual

All response to stimuli
apparent to the naked I.

Settle

All too many all too often do
aim too low and opt for any;
wait and want were hard to do.

Sex

To touch, taste, hear and see,
receptive to, and thrilled to be
with without and in-between,
open to, and emptying.

Shame

A shun by any other name
twists a child's wrist the same.

Shoe

Mountain climbing's more climactic,
with this global prophylactic.

Siamese

To be to a sibling wed,
a step behind, a head ahead.

Sideways

Doesn't mean a thing to me
in light of relativity.

Simile

Comparing aft and fore
like or as a metaphor.

Skeptic

One who does in place of gods,
put Fact and Not, which in their grace
they saw not fit to sort and sift,
into their proper place.

Snipe

To correspond without return,
removed from whom it does concern.

Snow

A fowl's flea a downy forest sees,
the sky a disco of frosted stained glass windows
beyond all hope of explanation,
falling sideways in formation.

Spoon

Adolescent protégé
to medieval trebuchet.

Sprain

Joint, muscle and tendon do
tend to mend when tended to.

Squircle

Squares which circle back abound,
where other squares are not around.

Street Sign

Tombstone to a spruce or pine
that could've stood the test of time.

Symbiosis

Giving and begetting,
neither taking nor regretting.

Table

A bit of whittle flat and still
held down by abdominal protrusion 'til
the meal is done and only bones remain,
dishes passing to another plane.

Tax

A bit of common profit kept aside,
in principle to profit you and I.

Television

A faucet dripping pungent waters
onto sponges: sons and daughters.

Temptation

To off and on and often see
what so ought, and oughtn't be.

Temptress

A she who hopes to help refrain
from every effort to abstain.

Therapist

Into darkened tunnel trains,
cutting teeth on broken brains.

Thermos

A vault if wanting in
and prison going out.

Thick

Wide, when something underneath resides.
If on the other outside it were found,
we would simply go around.

Thunder

I always hark to hear the arcs
of gigantic static sparks.

Thrust

To scooch upon a cooch when pelvic,
or sink a sword to redden velvet.

Time

A fib we sip with morning brew,
as if it's morning in Peru.

Together

Both to be, and coincide;
by and by, and I aside.

Tile

One quadrant in a grid of grout
you glued to kick the carpet out.

Tornado

It spins.   If we were spun we'd come undone.

Tragedy

Martyrs of a faith we have not named
put our grievances to shame.

Travel

Every place you've ever been
has never been the same again.

Tree

A root uprooted that believes,
it's not a root for having leaves.

Trimester

Awaren't, apparent, a parent.

Troll

To see a bridge and not to stroll;
instead to try to take a toll.

Twinge

A heartstring on a hook
that's hard to overlook.

Union

Lend a little muscle to
men who build, and break for you.

Universe

I cannot help but find absurd
the sum of all summed up
in just one word.

Vacuum

Just as lust and distance can attract,
a void deprived of substance too will act
as siren call to atoms passing near;
a quantum aphrodisiac.

Vagina

A theme park fit for men and women;
unbefitting infants to whom leaving is required,
and entrance is forbidden.

Vegan

Meat-eating bosses mean life losses
and vegans job security,
for in cannibal country we can't be canned
while canning at the cannery.

Verb

A home indeed for those in need
of a title to a deed.

Vibrator

A siege upon a castle gate
to breach a breach but then abate
should the captain of the cavalry
need a fresh replacement battery.

Villain

Every part completes the whole,
a hero made heroic
by each supporting role.

Vote

A decision made by wizened ones who had
hung their hopes for change on hanging chads.

War

Selected by those we elected,
representing our good will until
we willed to war, and good defected.

Waste

Potential which, once cast away
can be expressed a different way.

We

Said of a collective,
together or respective.

Weed

A plant un-wanted among your garden reeds,
though some may only shun the stems and seeds.

Wheel

That for which a lesson's meant
not to have to reinvent.

Withdraw

Seek to lest you peak abreast.

Wrapper

Alack, a lark of licking stopped
momentarily but oft,
to crop the crinkled top atop
a paper-padded lollipop.

Wrong

Everything and nothing seems perverse
given keen perspective or averse.
Depending who you question they will see
right or wrong in you or me.

X-Ray

Private doc and sunken socket do
adore a game of peek-a-boo.

Yell

To tersely talk in coarse vibration;
loosened by profuse libation.

Yellow

The primary way
to color one who runs away.

Young

Yet to be forgotten
or literally rotten.

Yours

That which I have yet to take
from within, and find it's mate.

Zombie

A corpse is a corpse of course,
but sometimes it's striped and a horse,
wandering by day,
saying nothing but "Grraaaaaaaaaaainsss...."
corpses of zorses in force.

Zen

To see all as good and bad,
and all that had to happen had.

Zygote

Heir apparent to a parent's wealth,
good fortune bid them give the gift of self.

I hope you enjoyed and continue to enjoy my book. If you do and did, check originalisbetter.com

No telling what you might find there.

www.ingramcontent.com/pod-product-compliance
Lightning Source LLC
Chambersburg PA
CBHW060426050426
42449CB00009B/2156